Giant Cranes

By Kenny Allen

Gareth Stevens
Publishing

Please visit our website, www.garethstevens.com. For a free color catalog of all our high-quality books, call toll free 1-800-542-2595 or fax 1-877-542-2596.

Library of Congress Cataloging-in-Publication Data

Allen, Kenny, 1971-
Giant cranes / Kenny Allen.
    p. cm. — (Monster machines)
Includes index.
ISBN 978-1-4339-7172-3 (pbk.)
ISBN 978-1-4339-7173-0 (6-pack)
ISBN 978-1-4339-7171-6 (library binding)
1. Cranes, derricks, etc.—Juvenile literature. I. Title.
TJ1363.A435 2012
621.8'73—dc23

                              2011044025

First Edition

Published in 2013 by
Gareth Stevens Publishing
111 East 14th Street, Suite 349
New York, NY 10003

Copyright © 2013 Gareth Stevens Publishing

Designer: Daniel Hosek
Editor: Greg Roza

Photo credits: Cover, p. 1 Shootov Igot/Shutterstock.com; p. 5 Danshutter/Shutterstock.com; p. 7 Vakhrushev Pavel/Shutterstock.com; p. 9 vesilvio/Shutterstock.com; p. 11 Flashon Studio/Shutterstock.com; p. 13 vnovikov/Shutterstock.com; p. 15 Yobidaba/Shutterstock.com; p. 17 corepics/Shutterstock.com; p. 19 jan kranendonk/Shutterstock.com; p. 21 Bloomberg/Getty Images.

Printed in the United States of America

CPSIA compliance information: Batch #CS12GS: For further information contact Gareth Stevens, New York, New York at 1-800-542-2595.

Contents

Time to Lift. 4

Rising High. 6

Ropes and Pulleys 8

Hoists. 10

Tower Cranes. 12

Truck Cranes 14

Overhead Cranes 16

Gantry Cranes 18

The Taisun Crane. 20

Glossary. 22

For More Information. 23

Index 24

Boldface words appear in the glossary.

Time to Lift

Cranes are used to lift heavy things. You may have seen a crane on a farm or at a **construction** site. Some cranes are on trucks. The tallest cranes help build skyscrapers. The strongest cranes help build giant **oil platforms**.

5

Rising High

Crane **frames** are called masts or towers. A mast reaches high into the sky. Many cranes also have a jib. A jib reaches out over the ground. This makes it easier for the crane to lift a load.

jib

mast

7

Ropes and Pulleys

Cranes use ropes or cables to lift things. Wheels called pulleys allow the rope to move smoothly. The rope sometimes has a hook on the end. The hook is used to hold on to heavy loads and lift them.

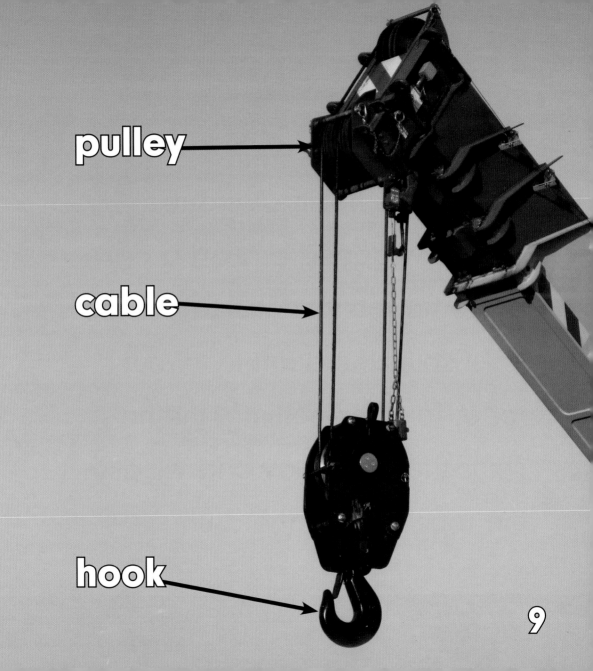

pulley

cable

hook

Hoists

Cranes use hoists. A crane's rope is wrapped around a part of the hoist called the **drum**. The hoist spins the drum to let out rope. To lift something, the hoist spins the other way and winds the rope around the drum.

Tower Cranes

Tower cranes often sit atop the tallest skyscrapers. They have long jibs to help lift heavy loads. When a tower crane needs to reach higher, it lifts itself up! Then workers add a new section to the tower.

13

Truck Cranes

Some cranes are on trucks. The frame of a truck-mounted crane is called a boom. Tow-truck cranes are small. However, some truck-mounted cranes are giant. The tallest truck-mounted crane can lift loads 47 stories into the sky!

15

Overhead Cranes

Overhead cranes don't have masts or booms. The hoist moves on an overhead beam. The beam moves on a set of tracks. The crane can pick up something on one side of a factory and move it to the other side.

17

Gantry Cranes

Gantry cranes are giant overhead cranes. The hoist moves back and forth on a beam, but the beam doesn't move. Instead, the entire crane moves on wheels or tracks. Gantry cranes lift giant **containers** off ships and put them onto trucks.

The Taisun Crane

The world's strongest crane is in China. The Taisun is a monster gantry crane. It is used to help build other monster machines, such as oil platforms. The Taisun holds the top three world records for the heaviest crane lifts!

The Amazing Taisun!

- **The Taisun crane is 374 feet (114 m) tall and 394 feet (120 m) wide.**

- **This gantry crane uses over 31 miles (50 km) of cable to lift objects.**

- **In April 2008, the Taisun crane lifted more than 20,000 metric tons (22,046 tons). That's about the same as 4,000 elephants!**

Glossary

construction: having to do with the act of building something

container: an object used to hold something

drum: a large spool used to wind up rope or cable

frame: something that holds up or gives shape to something else

oil platform: an oil drilling rig at sea

For More Information

Books

Askew, Amanda. *Cranes*. Irvine, CA: QEB Publishing, 2010.

Star, Fleur. *Crane*. New York, NY: Dorling Kindersley, 2005.

Websites

How Hydraulic Cranes Work

science.howstuffworks.com/transport/engines-equipment/hydraulic-crane.htm

Learn about a different kind of truck-mounted crane.

How Tower Cranes Work

science.howstuffworks.com/transport/engines-equipment/tower-crane.htm

Read more about tower cranes and see these amazing machines at work.

Index

beam 16, 18
boom 14, 16
cables 8, 9, 21
construction site 4
containers 18
drum 10
factory 16
farm 4
gantry cranes 18, 20, 21
hoists 10, 16, 18
hook 8, 9
jib 6, 7, 12
load 6, 8, 12, 14

mast 6, 7, 16
oil platforms 4, 20
overhead cranes 16, 18
pulleys 8, 9
ropes 8, 10
skyscrapers 4, 12
Taisun crane 20, 21
tower 6
tower cranes 12
tracks 16, 18
truck cranes 14
trucks 4, 14, 18
world records 20